THAT
THE ROCK

rita mæ brown

Illustrations
ginger legato

Dedicated to women everywhere.

The Hand
That Cradles
The Rock

Diana Press

Oakland, California

Library of Congress Cataloging in Publication Data

Brown, Rita Mae.
    The hand that cradles the rock.

    Poems.
    I. Title.
PS3552.R698H3 1974   811'.5'4   74-13602
ISBN 0-88447-005-9

Typeset, printed and bound by Diana Press, Inc., 4400 Market St., Oakland, Ca. 94608. Single and bulk orders available by mail from Diana Press.

Introduction

Diana Press is pleased to be making available in paperback *The Hand that Cradles the Rock*. This is the first published collection of Rita Mae Brown's poetry, and although written prior to 1971, we feel these poems have never received the circulation among women that they deserve. In re-reading this book, some three years after I first saw it, I am again struck with the power of its imagery and language.

Rita Mae works out of a tradition of carefully structured language and form. Similarly, recurrent images and themes run throughout the book. In the illustrations Ginger Legato has made visual two of those themes: the sea and death.

Death and destruction are repeatedly connected with male culture and men. Sometimes their violence against individual women is described as in "For Lydia French". Sometimes their destruction touches all of nature as in "On The Rooftop Where All The Pigeons Go To Die" and "The Invisible Sovereign". The words that recur—bones, decomposed, dirge, stillborn, skulls, sterile, broken—bring us sharply against the reality of our culture. A culture which plunders nature and robs people of their connection with it—"Beauty, the people want beauty." The United States (Cygne) and New York City in particular are the epitome of the inhuman, harsh man-made landscape—"We fall among the skyscrapers/To perish without light."

In contrast, the sea recalls nature and a return to beautiful, living, growing beings. Women are associated with the ocean—"But I/Return to the ocean/Rolling centuries in a kiss." Many of the love poems to women—and there are an astonishing number of very good ones—come back to the sea. "Silently we are cementing our lives/As a coral reef is built/Blossoming into iridescence/Providing homes for wandering Angel fish/And other bits of beauty." Water as refreshing and and nourishing, ever-changing and yet unchanging is the abode of women, akin to their very nature.

The stance of woman in the midst of male destruction is one of defiance. She refuses to give in and looks forward to her day of vengeance—"We grew a strong and bitter root/That promises justice." She sees the hope of women in their ministering to each other— "We must hunt as wounded women/The balm to heal one another." And even when wounded to the death, she dies on the run, uncowed and unbowing.

The longest and most complete poem in the book is "The New Lost Feminist." In it Rita Mae combines the separate themes—a destructive and dying culture, suffering womanhood, and hope for the future—into one unified whole. I would like to excerpt a description of that poem published in *The Furies*, February, 1972:

"Central to the impact of *The Hand that Cradles the Rock* is the poem, "The New Lost Feminist", which is constructed in the form of a triptych (a picture having three compartments, two of which fold over the middle one which is fixed). The beginning quote from *Alice in Wonderland* sets the mood for the poem. It is the cold recognition of an awful societal truth.

"The left panel is the expression of the deep personal frustration, powerlessness and suffering of a woman. It is about the horrible mutilation that has been done by a bondage made of empty words and promises and deceit. The words are carefully chosen to convey the feeling of utter destruction that has been done to the woman: "incoherent", "bleed", "gushing broken participles". The first seven lines are a remarkable selection of words that really give a painfully vivid description of the end of a desperate fight to stay alive and unconquered. In the next two lines, the trivial concerns of those who abandon her ("chatter", "small change", "prefixes and suffixes") are juxtaposed with the enormity of their consequence: the woman is dying.

"The center panel gives the societal picture. The country where the judges of the highest court have so little understanding of human needs (in the same breath, they judge lollipops—a real Supreme Court case—and women) that they are described as children. But it is the "twilight" of the Supreme Court, and "Goliath" (the world of corporate business is dealt with in one blow) is staggering. We can expect a fall. The oppressed people, uncorrupted and beautiful in this poem, are fleeing the land. America is dying, and the words chosen for the last five lines of the second stanza make the reader feel physical disgust at the ugly scene. But before the end comes, the cause of death is made clear: the demise of the system was part of the nature of the system itself.

"The right panel is a recognition of what has been done to us by the society and what we have to do about it. The beast that follows us is the ruling man, the male supremacist. His presence is sometimes illusive—a shadow that blends with our own, without our fully realizing it. And it divides us; it pits woman against woman. But perhaps there was a time when women did not derive their identity from men, and when the shadow of the beast did not plague ours. We don't know for sure. Oppression has been so great for so long that it is hard to know whether we have a golden age to return to.

"The last stanza is exciting. We begin to really feel the weight of centuries through the beat, the sound, and the meaning of the words: "limping", "crippled", "dragging", "heavy", "submission", "sorrow". The spell is broken quickly, sharply. And we have the answer: "It's time to break and run." "

We hope this poetry helps you "break and run."

Coletta Reid

Contents

On The Rooftop
Where All The Pigeons Go To Die

A Litany for the Male Culture

Ghosts of pigeons police their bones
And forgotten feathers bejewled as
   white spiders spin in memory of
   starboard lights and phosphorescent tortoises;
Before great hulks of decomposed intelligence
   bobbled on the Hudson flowing endlessly
   to the wastelands of the sea,
Before dirtied seagulls with leather lungs had
   sung a dirge for the passing of pigeons
   and the senseless slaughter of insects,
Before universities and warmakers fed off each other
   like incestuous crabs;
When grasshoppers hoarded sunshine
   and sang of tulips, fat and fine,
Before a battleship passed behind my spine,

When magnificent morning glories praised the days
Before the Titanic sailed beneath the waves,
   lights ablaze,
Showing ice fish threading a sunken temple of Jupiter's
   ancient encrusted marble maze.
Now triplets of nucleotides dance in their head
They dig subways to ignore the pigeon dead.

The pigeons fly low
Wing tip to wing tip they haunt the sky
Above the businessman and my naked eye.
The wasp, unmoved, stuffs her nest with paralyzed spiders.
Frogs prophesy in the name of the Great Blue Light.
Solar winds clash with the night
Rats, afraid, run beneath the Milky Way.
Some lost dinosaur is crawling out a blistering egg
To hunt her heir unto this day.

Men fall into doubt
Clutching it in lieu of the truth.

For Joan
Bird

Her name hangs heavy on my lips
In long nights I dream
A bright ringed hallucination
I reach and find her taken.

Necropolis

These sanctified vegetables
Stunted fruits in fallow fields,
Eunuchs, caricatured human beings,
These scholars
Translating ignorance into Latin and Greek;
Tittering over beds long rotted to earth,
Endlessly dissecting the cadaver of a nun.
These secure hypocrites
Embalmed in an equinox of vanity.
Lead on! Lead on! Lead on!
How easy to be king
When all your subjects are dead.
Archaelogical beings
Preserved in penultimate time.
Drone, drone
Drone your dreary dithyrambs
You stillborn, celibate intellects.
You fools, you frauds
You accumulated postules of useless learning.
Damned as mummified moles burrowing feverishly
Under Cheops immobile sands
The curse of the makers upon you.

Radical
Man

Witness his ego
How it flies
Up from earth
Seeing no other
In rarefied atmosphere
It congratulates itself
On its epoxied excellence,
The Eternal I,
A marvelous me of malevolence
Such is my brother
Such is our age.

The
Disconnection

Strings lay all about
She told me
Strings and threads lay all about
And none of them connected
Or touched her outstretched hand.
She held out her hand to me,
It seems a year behind
She held out her hand
And I reached back with mine.
But the strings and threads tied up her brain
And she cried in anguish
She cried my name
Let go my hand to cradle her head
And now she sits alone
She sits and cradles her head
Afraid that it will roll away.
Too tired to cut it off.

For Men Only

I took him in
I can say no more
I took him in
And he lived there and died
A creature of time.
While I
Like the tide
Washed him in wave
After wave of eternity
That he might understand immortality
    before he goes
To the grave.
All men must die.
But I
Return to the ocean
Rolling centuries in a kiss
And lap at the moon
Until the eye of god
or locusts
Fix us
 Still.

The
Etruscan
Queen

Inspects ancient bathrooms
See how she goes
Through Tuscan tidbits
Climbing dusty orgasms
To the touch of an archaic crotch
Long discarded underpants,
Holy vestige, pre-Roman relic
What joy. What knowledge. What truth.
"Oh and did you know
their shoes changed to pointed toe
around 550 B.C., can you see?"
She troubles herself about Etruscan clothes,
"Did their whores wear red hose?"
We costume our poor to hide their rags
She wonders were there well dressed fags.

For Sweet
Ellen

Sometime I look at you and wonder
How was it you
Were pulled under
And not myself?
Trapped in an undertow of pea-green rooms,
Fourteen months you were coming up
From the sea of the mind drowned;
Coming to the beach
Where I
The first amphibian
Was moving unused legs.

"A case of jam tomorrow and never jam today."

Alice in Wonderland

The New
Lost Feminist
A Triptych

The Left Panel:

Incoherent in the midst of men
I bleed at the mouth
Gushing broken participles
And teeth cracked on bullet words.
I bleed for want of a single, precious word,
Dying in the network of swollen blue veins
Large with my life force.
How can you turn away and chatter in your small change
Of prefixes and suffixes?
A woman is dying for want of a single unrealized word,
Freedom.

The Center Panel:

In the twilight of the Supreme Court
Wrinkled robed children
Passed judgement on Whistling lollipops and women.
Goliath staggers, his briefcase hemorrhaging with deals.
The Court hears the last appeal
For a land where means do not devour ends.

The underground railway smuggles giant blacks and
Glistening women to hidden empires beneath the polar caps.
America's rotting rib cage frames the gallows
Of her putrid goals.
How the nation rolls to stand on its feet
An upturned crab as decayed as its prey.
The young vomit and turn away.

Underground stations fill with blacks,
Women and the young
Fleeing a Troy that has built its own horse
America becomes a bloated corpse.

The Right Panel:

How this beast follows us
His leprous shadow blending with our own
And we fall to fighting among ourselves
Clawing the silk cheeks of other women.

Was there a golden age to remember?
Was there a time when we knew our name
And called up great cities within us,
Our voices ringing out tidings of future nations?
Did we walk past ziggarats then as now
Heads bowed, shameful as a conquered race?
Was there ever a time?

Women, women limping on the edges of the History of Man
Crippled for centuries and dragging the heavy emptiness
Past submission and sorrow to forgotten and unknown selves.
It's time to break and run.

"A silver crab on mica sands
Sideways she moves toward a bleeding sun."

RMB

Canto Cantare
Cantavi Cantatum

I sing of a woman and summer
Of hot days within my limbs
July of months and blazing woman
Who comes before me, burning, burning
Whose eyes stir sulfer seas inside
To collide with the shores of silence.
I sing of a woman and summer
The woman loves another:
I burn as a lonely taper
In blackest night.

Rhadamanthos

Love knows no justice
Fruits fall from trees
An overripe tangerine
Entertains merry ants
Is a love to the hands
That never took it from the tree.

The
Midnight
Caesura

At the end of the afternoon
She kindly disengaged me
Or was I abandoned?
No matter what the term,
She let me go
Alone to my bed
Where her name is sewn
Along the edges of my dreams.

Fire
Island

The sea is obsidian
The sea is jade
The sea is a thousand Iroquois arrowheads
Piercing the shore.
My body is borne over the sea
I move on the backs of fishes
Swimming toward an island of cannibals
Ravenous for large, juicy genitals.
My body rises and my body falls
Listing toward the open air asylum,
Where I, as a woman
Shall walk on the bones of men
Ignoring the sacramental siphoned skull
Whose capped and sterile teeth
Whisper the great lie, "Love."

Bullseye
The Epoch Begins July 20, 1969

Lions' teeth lay yellow in the grass
Along with the eye of the day
Impaled on milken spikes.
A year throbs in a rib cage.
Phantom Incas and Aztecs calculate upon great golden calendars
Trapping time between betrayed stars.
And men pretend to grow
According to the sequence of Arabic numerals
Beat out in the prisoner's rhymic thrashing.

Dead men climb pyramids to read the sky
And pray for the female centaur
Whose great and curved bow
Lets fly the arrow
To pin the millenium like a poisonous eagle
To a rotted tree.

A thousand years is as a day
When murderers manipulate timetables
Set for planetary rape.
Woman, put your ear to your breast.
Hoofbeats.

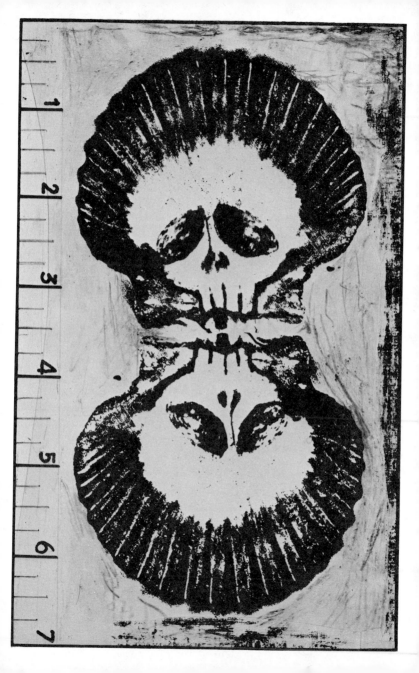

Being

Should she leave me
I, as a bee
Stepped on and stinging
Try to fly
Spining out my entrails
To sputter and die
Soft guts superimposed
Upon the uninterested sky.
Smashed as all images must be
And the bee
Falls back to earth
Not far from her sting
A tiny black and yellow bundle
Her transparent wings
Nervously beating life's last pulses
Wings on which life and love etched
Opposing answers
To the question outlined by the soft coil
Of her insides
Spread along the ground.

New York
City

Smokestacks point at polluted skies
Amputated fingers stuck in our eyes,
Great glass altars stand in precision
Singing stacatto hymns to corporate vision.

An awesome jewel
An awesome jewel
Awaiting the Second Coming
Any second coming.

We come to Manhattan
We come bent with mortality
We come to catch sight of a flawed diamond
Aflame with imperfection
Red with blood and the sun
And still we come
Spat out like seed pods
Driven toward hard ground
We fall among the skyscrapers
To perish without light
And still we come
To see a city sanctified in emphatic communion
Millions of unwatered sinners withering together,
The human reunion.

"Now, gods,
          stand up
     for bastards!"
                    Edmund
Act I, Scene II, King Lear

Orphans cling to a country
As children to a father
There's no love but still it's home
As you leave in wider and wider circles
Turning to where the center should be,
Amerika.
You find him, syphlitic whore
An international festering sore.

Original Sin

This hand behind my back
Holding the other
As if some brother
Clutching its partner in crime,
The sins of the right hand.
Ten tight witnesses
Interlocking,
A hung jury
Locked in the fingers of indecision
As a hand fills a hand
In loneliness
Its other;
Awaiting, awaiting another.

The Twentyfirst
Century

Let me go
From this day forward
Brighter than one thousand suns
Proclaiming love
Without a word.
There are no bottoms to words,
The bottoms have fallen out
Broken cups
Too cheap to hold, "I love you,"
The bottoms have fallen out of words
And cloak-like I cover you
Catching the honey from your lips and thighs
Where love lies.
Holding you
While language collapses around us.
I love you is on touching tongues
Silent in their meeting.
With this communion now,
Let me go
From this day forward
Brighter than one thousand suns
Lighting the way for you alone.
Lost searchers for the Holy Grail will
Follow us into the Twentyfirst Century.

To
My Wife

Who is not my wife
Nor bound to me by paper
Nor am I to her
Bound as husband or wife.
I call her, Wife,
A paltry proper noun
Trying to encompass
"Until death us do part."

Silently we are cementing our lives
As a coral reef is built
Blossoming into iridescence
Providing homes for wandering Angel fish
And other bits of beauty.
Like the reefs
When we ourselves have died
The skeletons of our life work
Will still give homes to sea orphans
Swimming in waters of absurdity.

Dancing
The Shout To The True
Gospel

Or: The Song My Movement Sisters Won't Let Me Sing

I follow the scent of a woman
Melon heavy
Ripe with joy
Inspiring me
To rip great holes in the night
So the sun blasts through.
And this is all I shall ever know:
Her breath
Filling the hollows of my neck
A luxury diminishing death.

Hymn To The 10,000 Who Die Each Year On The Abortionist's Table In Amerika

Let us make death masks
And run our fingers over them
Searching
In the crevices of the slain faces
For slivers of truth
Which prick our fingers
Drawing blood to the sunlight
Though painful in its pushing
We must hunt as wounded women
The balm to heal one another.

The Invisible
Sovereign

I have sat upon this pile of broken bottles
Feeling the pain no longer
Until I shift my weight
And am cut anew.
As blind men fear glass
I fear and find myself amid the terror,
A forest of frightening familiars.
Blind go I
But for her voice
Calling me through a smashed world
And calling up the awesome world within me.
Strangely, she stops now and then.
And you can see me, unseeing
Perched atop this decomposed glass city
Like some emaciated scarecrow
Ravaged by ulcerous holes within
Where a world once was,
Listening, listening.

The New
Litany

Compounded in confusion
A mute, prosaic Sappho, I pray
"Oh let me dumb be blessed with song
To fling at the metaphors of darkness
Cemented in silence of swift time
On this side of morning;
To bring the dawn and rein Time's ravenous mouth,
To spend the sacraments on sheets
Redeemed in a kiss,
To proclaim New Christmas
The carol chanted by her eyes."
All this splendor, I pray
A groundling with face upturned
To the snow fallen down
In the night of her hair
Above me.
Deaf to my song?
Would she feign deafness
Or wave me away?
Ah, I'm left to pray,
As Venus in her ascendency
Draws triangulations on reality.

Love On The Run
or The
Trackshoe Sonata

Ask me

Do I love her?

I would have to answer,

Yes.

For I have smelled laughter

Lurking in the folds of her dress,

I have felt her hard beating and half mended heart

And sang litanies upon her breast.

Ask me,

Do I love her?

Yes, yes, yes.

Song Of
My Wealth

I shall whisper in the nautilis of your ear
Songs of dolphins dying in Floridean seas
Reborn as jewel encrusted pins
Poised, surfaced in the windows of Tiffany and Sons
So far from my reach.
But let me take you to the cool sands continually cleaned
By scuttling claws of chambermaid crabs,
Where tiny birds with invisible knees stoop to pick what they missed.
Schools of night fish flash fire under the moon
Synchronized silver on a string
Pursued by a steel-blue rapier
Barracuda that knifes through jetties
Grinning in his rows of terrible sharp teeth.
A manta ray flaps his wide wings
Slow in his slender beauty
And the moon slides over the upturned tips
Spreading light over all
Clothing us in splendid silver garments
As we lay naked
Amid stars and starfish and shooting stars within us.
There open the oyster of myself
Wherein the blood pearl was a long time making
A piece of suffering enameled to joy.
Take it
This pearl
This soul which never wanders
Let others gaze in store front windows
Take it.

Song Of
A Poor
Young Woman

White feathered palms tremble
Beneath my spreading fingertips
I'm line with mother-of-pearl
Silver snails with opal tails
Slide beneath my skull
My bones are gilded and slim.
Emeralds and topaz hide behind my eyes
Unblinking before all earth
Sapphire lizards send fire along my tongue
And I burn for centuries unborn.

A Journey Into
The Eyeless
Sockets Of The Night

This is the day of my majority
This is the day I,
Dying, plowed the sea
And planted dead trees,
Feeling my youth go through my fingers
Like a razor to the bone.
I have come to the threshold of pain
An unwilling bride
Carried by pride
Across the jaws of broken promises
To bear in this depth, sorrow.
Should I die in childbirth
They will call it suicide
As I cry for one finger of the dawn.

The Female
Of The
Species

Like the lioness wounded, disconsolate
I roar and bend the grasses
Driving tender antelopes
Through hushed savannahs
So none may scent the side's deepening wound
Lions listen in the pride, cowed
As the lioness lopes a hardened silhouette
Across the cruel and lovely plain
To die on the run.

The Middle Class
Identity Crisis
Viewed Through The Eyes Of
Poor White Trash

I am not the same
I am not the same,
Where is the name behind my name?
The laugh behind my lips?
My faces's secret is reflected
Bouncing back from broken mirrors
Fragments of an inoffensive caricature
Fused into a patchwork quilt of being.

The anguish of fall
Sent inarticulate sorrow
Far within the bone.
A ship's horn on the Hudson
Announced winter's advent
Leaves bend their knees
Out of respect
For the dying grass
And I walk home alone.

Aristophanes'
Symposium

I have known it from the beginning
As though by fate
Disbelieving fate.
That we as one
Were divided by some awful hand
And I have searched the centuries for your face,
Hearing eons echo your name,
A muffled refrain drenched in longing.
Long have I yearned,
Spurning women
All women save the one I knew
In thick clouds of prehistory.
Even Helen was a bone
I threw to Paris
Outraged at her imperfection.
I toiled, a plaything of Cronos
From Genesis through silly flocks of years
Herding decades into the penumbra of my brain
Poking shadows of bleating days for your face.
The years slipped by
And I alone felt them go
No longer counting sheep
Too tired for counting sheep
But I will know you as you know me
And one day you will call me, "Woman."

A Song
For Winds
And My
Vassar Women

Here among the trees
The world takes the shape of a woman's body
And there is beauty in the place
Lips touch
But minds miss the vital connection
And hearts wander
Down dormitory halls
More hurt than hollow.

The Self
Affirms
Herself

Neither stars nor gods can guide me
A law unto myself
And a self apart
I move in the shadow of the great guillotine
That rhythmically does its work
On heads remaining unbowed.

The
Bourgeois
Questions

"I wonder about the burn
Behind your eyes,
What is it in you that disquiets me so?
Do you hate me for my softness?"

"No, I've come through a land
You'll never know."

The Arrogance Of Immortality

The difference between
My little cat
And I
Is
That I
Know
I am going to die.

Cygne

Sings the swan
Her song of aching beauty
Neck outstretched to question the sky
Then coils and pierces her breast
That houses the song.
So sing I
"Amerika, Amerika."

Horse
Sense

Summer smolders
And days draw long
Grapevines roll to the sea,
I ride through a field of Queen Anne's lace,
Heather and blue pine,
Come kind horse and lead the way
To beach plums, life and immortal play.

For Lydia
French

Shot and killed, August 13, 1970

Women know
Women have always known
As marrow to the bone
Death is at the heart of men.

I touch your solitary, senseless death
And run for my life.
Men shall yet know
The fruits earned
Of death.
Goodbye, Lydia

The
President's
Bedchamber

He lies awake at night
With his hand over his heart
Because he is not sure
If it's still there.

The Great
Pussblossom

Hoisting her tail to the vertical
Pussblossom plants a kiss of suspicion upon her spouse,
"Tell me, dear, have you been eating mouse?"

Clytemnestra's
Song

He yielded to me
And I felt his body
Go under mine
Like an enemy last conquered.
What ecstasy, a just death!

A
Short Note
For Liberals

I've seen your kind before
Forty plus and secure
Settling for a kiss from feeble winds
And calling it a storm.

Macho

The lamplites are lite with blood
How can we find our way home
Where mother washes our agony and
Hangs it on the line to dry?
In these times is it proper for men to cry?

The Marriage Hearse

Tell me the story of your love
And how it died
Like worn winds torn on
Winter's jagged branches.
How you, found the lie
Deep within the kiss.

History
Reappears
In The Dead
Of Night

I dreamed I spoke in foreign tongues
Thick liqueurs
Dark as the dawn,
Oh, Bysantium.

Sunset

I ride in Central Park
To see the buildings rise
Like dusty rose madonnas
Lifting huge shoulders to the sky
I ride and say farewell
To a city doomed to die.

The
Women's
House Of
Detention

Here amid the nightsticks, handcuffs and interrogation
Inside the cells, beatings, the degradation
We grew a strong and bitter root
That promises justice.

Song Of
The Subway

There is a longing in the subway
Rising from the damp sour tracks
Seizing our nostrils until they ache.
Beauty, the people want beauty.

Past our longing speeds the empty train
Headlights smashed and whistle shrill
A ghost train shuttling to a caterpillar's grave.
The people watch, silent and still.

Overhead, business men carry laundry bags
Filled with dirty dreams.
Will the train never come?
Beauty, the people want. . . . . .

Promittor

Dew falls on the oysters at low tide
And the sea is ablaze with pearls.
I ride a horse to moongate
Where the water's fire
Lights the backbones of prehistoric fish
Tangled in my brain.

The
Nihilist

I know nothing
Neither life nor death
Yet I live
Brutalized, stupid, dumb
I live to cling
To climb
To cry, "I am."

For
Madam
Binh

The birds bow before me
And dogs mourne my step
Such is my anguish
Such, my despair.
The pure who plunder not
Are butchered, stripped and left to rot.

Elle

Someone wrote in French
"Where are the snows of yesteryear?"
And I reply in English
"In my heart, in my heart."

The Awakening

Men's arteries are turning to stone.
The owl of Athena takes wing
Only at dusk
And brushes the eyelids of Amazons
Who soldier their shields
And promise fresh blood
To make the trees grow
From dead sparrows' throats.

St·Zita's Home
For Friendless
Women

The unwed

Eyes downcast

Pass each other like

Dumb cargo ships

Sailing over dirty tile floors

Eyeless as their unborn

They ignore each other

And steam to watery graves.

Sappho's
Reply

My voice rings down through thousands of years
To coil around your body and give you strength,
You who have wept in direct sunlight,
Who have hungered in invisible chains,
Tremble to the cadence of my legacy:
An army of lovers shall not fail.

Feminist

Having slumbered
She rose and shook
Victorian shadows from her hair.

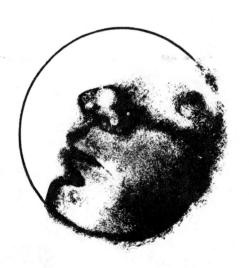